T0191235

POCKET STUDY SKILLS

Series Editor: **Kate Williams**, *Oxford Brookes University, UK*
Illustrations by Sallie Godwin

For the time-pushed student, the *Pocket Study Skills* pack a lot of advice into a little book. Each guide focuses on a single crucial aspect of study giving you step-by-step guidance, handy tips and clear advice on how to approach the important areas which will continually be at the core of your studies.

Published

14 Days to Exam Success (2nd edn)
Analyzing a Case Study
Brilliant Writing Tips for Students
Completing Your PhD
Doing Research (2nd edn)
Getting Critical (2nd edn)
Managing Stress
Planning Your Dissertation (2nd edn)
Planning Your Essay (2nd edn)
Planning Your PhD
Posters and Presentations

Reading and Making Notes (2nd edn)
Referencing and Understanding Plagiarism (2nd edn)
Reflective Writing
Report Writing (2nd edn)
Science Study Skills
Studying with Dyslexia (2nd edn)
Success in Groupwork
Time Management
Where's Your Argument?
Writing for University (2nd edn)

POCKET STUDY SKILLS

Lucinda Becker

14 DAYS TO EXAM SUCCESS

SECOND EDITION

© Lucinda Becker, under exclusive licence to Springer Nature Limited, 2010, 2018

All rights reserved. No reproduction, copy or transmission of this publication may be made without written permission.

No portion of this publication may be reproduced, copied or transmitted save with written permission or in accordance with the provisions of the Copyright, Designs and Patents Act 1988, or under the terms of any licence permitting limited copying issued by the Copyright Licensing Agency, Saffron House, 6–10 Kirby Street, London EC1N 8TS.

Any person who does any unauthorized act in relation to this publication may be liable to criminal prosecution and civil claims for damages.

The author has asserted her right to be identified as the author of this work in accordance with the Copyright, Designs and Patents Act 1988.

First edition 2010
Second edition 2018
First published 2010 by
PALGRAVE

Palgrave in the UK is an imprint of Springer Nature Limited, registered in England, company number 785998, of 4 Crinan Street, London, N1 9XW.

Palgrave® is a registered trademark in the United States, the United Kingdom, Europe and other countries.

ISBN 978–1–352–00371–0 paperback

This book is printed on paper suitable for recycling and made from fully managed and sustained forest sources. Logging, pulping and manufacturing processes are expected to conform to the environmental regulations of the country of origin.

A catalogue record for this book is available from the British Library.

A catalog record for this book is available from the Library of Congress.

Contents

Getting started

What is the point of revision?

This might sound like a question with a ridiculously obvious answer: *I am revising so that I will succeed in my exams*. In fact, you will be doing much more than that as you work through this book, almost without knowing it. As you prepare for an exam using this guide, you will be making the very best use of your time by developing your skills, deepening your understanding, and learning to analyse a situation and express yourself (these last two are, of course, key to success in your future career).

By using this book, you have demonstrated that you are committed to achieving the best exam results you can in the time available to you. As you work through it, there are a few key principles to remember:

- What you know is often less important than how effectively you use that knowledge.
- By reworking and using material, as this guide suggests, you will be deepening your understanding, which means that you are not just remembering information, but learning as you revise.

- Whenever you start to revise, there is always something you can do to improve your results and boost your learning.
- *However*, knowing when to stop is also important – your mind and body need rest.
- Recognising your learning style, and the best revision techniques for you, will help you to develop as a student.
- Understanding how different exams work is important – knowing what is really being asked of you is crucial.

Smarter learning

You will notice that both 'learning' and 'memorising' are mentioned in this guide. As you are gearing up to exams, your primary focus, understandably, will be on memorising information and then using it in the most productive way in order to succeed. You will also, depending on the type of exam, be acquiring a set of skills that will help you in your future learning, as well as in the exam itself. On Day One we will be considering different sorts of exams and the skills you will need to succeed.

Making use of the information you have is the best way to recall it in an exam, but it is also a great way to learn. As you make plans, see patterns and reduce material to the essentials, you are making judgements that will not only be reinforcing the work you have already done on your course, but will also be helping you move forward. You will notice patterns you did not spot in the classroom or lecture hall, and you will see connections across courses and topics that could not have been clear to you earlier.

All of this will happen as we work through your revision together, but recognising this now, at the outset, will help you to maximise the long-term advantages to be gained from this experience. You do not have to see 'revision time' as something separate that comes after your 'learning time'. Instead, take a moment every now and then and think about what is happening to you – there are 'smarter learning' prompts to help you with this throughout the book.

In the fourteen days before your exams, you can make a huge difference. If you have longer than two weeks, you can take more time to complete each day's task, but a fortnight will be enough time to marshal the facts and ideas and make use of them so that you improve your performance radically.

Take it steady: for each day there is a checklist of things to do, an extended section that covers a key aspect of exam preparation, and a page or so that offers you some extra help and support as you move forward. You will not need to produce a revision timetable – this book does that for you – but you will need to set aside time each day to work through the tasks set out here.

How to use this book ...

Success in exams is not just about what you know: it is also about how you use what you know. This book is designed to help you remember as much as you can, but also to use that knowledge in the most effective way.

Unplanned revision can be deathly dull, and that is not conducive to remembering what you need to recall in an exam. By following the plan for each day, you will keep your brain active and geared up to perform in the exams. By varying your tasks and actively using your knowledge, you will be in the best position possible as you move towards the exams.

You will notice that this guide relies on hard-copy work – revision cards, hand-drawn plans and suchlike. This does not mean that you cannot produce some or all of this material in electronic form, but it comes with a warning: most of us recall information and patterns better if we can see them in our own handwriting, and the very act of writing something out is often a constructive part of the process of learning and memorising. However, if you know that you recall things more clearly on screen or in typewritten text, then use the method that works best for you.

For the first five days of your revision you will be sorting and storing information – this will give you the material you need to make a good impression in the exam. After that, you will be using your stored information to produce exam and test plans until Day Ten, when you will focus more tightly on the exam, giving yourself some mock exams. Day Eleven is an easier day, and then you will take a run-up to the exams with a structured series of tasks.

The key to success is to keep going in those first few days. Think of it like a construction project. You are taking down the wall of information, brick by brick, discarding some bricks you do not need and reassembling the bricks into a new shape for the exam.

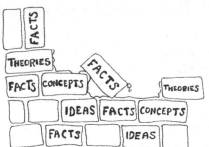

Things to do today

❑ Look through sample exam papers or online practice tests for your course, so that you know where you are going. You might have been given some examples, or you might find them in the library or on the website for your university or college.

❑ Make sure that you are clear about the division of marks between coursework and exams. This may vary from course to course. Although you will want to shine in every exam, you might feel less pressured if you discover that the exam for a particular course only counts for 30% of the mark; if it counts for 100% of the mark for one course, your focus will be far greater on that portion of revision.

❑ Check and double-check the exam timetable and put copies of it in your diary, on your fridge door – anywhere and everywhere you can.

❑ Divide your material into eight sections, taking into account how much material you need to cover for each of your courses, and how much credit attaches to each. You might bring two small courses together in one section of material, or divide a particularly challenging or important course into two or more sections of material. If you are preparing for an exam in just one or two courses, you will divide each course into several sections of material. Do not worry that some sections of material will seem 'easier' than others: that will give you some easier days as you progress, which is a good thing.

❑ Eight sections will give you the division of material you need to work through the revision process in fourteen days; if you have more or less time than that, you can make more or fewer sections of material.

How your learning style can help you

You may already know your preferred learning style. If not, it is a good idea to think about it now. There are many theories about learning styles and the impact they have, but for the purposes of your revision you might like to consider these:

If your style is …	
Visual	… you like to revise by using images, so you might prepare a plan that you can glance at, rather than a list of facts. You prefer to learn by seeing things rather than hearing.
Aural	… you prefer to revise by hearing, so you might choose to record your key revision cards on your phone and then play them back, or you might need to read key facts aloud before they lodge firmly in your mind. You enjoy someone explaining something to you.

If your style is ...	
Verbal	... you prefer words to images, so you will enjoy making revision cards and will probably revise in silence. You enjoy learning by reading.
Kinaesthetic	... you like activity as you learn, and so might benefit hugely from walking around a room as you work through your revision cards. You enjoy learning activities that allow you to move, even a little. You prefer not just to sit in one place to study.
Logical	... you enjoy systems and a logical flow of argument. It is likely that you have already chosen to study a subject that allows you to rely on flowcharts as a means of planning and revising. You find learning much easier if you are shown in diagrammatic form how facts flow from one point to the next.
Social	... you would find revision lonely and difficult by yourself and so are more likely to spend at least some of your time in a revision group, either in person or online. You enjoy groupwork learning and find that sharing ideas with fellow students really helps you.
Solitary	... you would be more likely to find that a revision group gets in your way; you will probably choose to prepare for an exam by yourself. Your best learning happens when you are reflecting on it once you are alone.

As you can see, your learning style will affect how well different activities can support your learning, so getting this right now will help you as you move forward.

> **⟫ Smarter learning**
>
> *There are plenty of free online tests you can take to discover your preferred learning style (bearing in mind that most of us can benefit from most of these styles to some extent), but you could also take a little time now to think about how you prefer to learn and revise. This will help you throughout your studying life.*

Types of exam

The type of exam you are facing will affect the way you revise and the skills you will need to develop, so here is some guidance.

Multiple-choice exams

In a multiple-choice exam you will face, for each question, a set of answers, of which you must usually choose just one. For revision, this means learning as many facts and ideas as possible. You also need to understand how multiple-choice tests tend to work.

For any set of possible answers, there will usually be one that is fairly obviously false, several that are plausible but not right, and one or two that look correct. The secret is to take the time to examine these last two possibilities closely so that you choose the right one. In the exam, you do not have to answer the questions in order. Instead, you could work through the paper, choosing the answers to the questions you find easiest, then spending longer on the more difficult questions. Try not to rush the first stage: it is too easy to tick the wrong box in your haste; leave yourself more time than you might usually do to check your answers: the speed of these exams can easily catch you out.

For this type of exam you need to develop the ability to make judgements under pressure. Practice multiple-choice tests are going to be important in your preparation. You could also hone this skill online, with any game that requires quick thinking and speedy reactions, but remember that you are aiming to take enough time to understand each question and to check your answers – judgement is as important as speed.

Short-answer exams

In a short-answer exam you will need fewer facts at your fingertips than in a multiple-choice exam, but you will have to know how to plan precisely and write succinctly. Your plan for each answer might not be as elaborate as for a full essay exam – perhaps just a set of bullet points – but it will be essential if you are not to get carried away and to find that you have spent too long on one answer and included too much material. Some students prefer to write their answers using bullet points, too, so that they remain clear and precise in their writing. If that is how you prefer to write in this type of exam, make sure in advance that using bullet points is acceptable.

You are mastering two key skills for this type of exam: the ability to manage your time and the ability to choose the most relevant material to support the points or argument you are making. You can help yourself here by making sure that you only have the essential information on your revision cards (more on these later) and that you make plenty of 'connections cards' – you are given an example of this type of revision card on Day Two.

Essay exams

These are perhaps the most traditional exams, asking for one or more essays in two or three hours. The good news is that they require, funnily enough, the least amount of knowledge. Instead, they ask you to use your knowledge in answering questions. You will be showing how well you understand the area you are discussing, how familiar you are with all aspects of a topic (or several topics) and how well you can develop an argument that will depend on your skills in critical analysis. Planning and practice will be crucial, and learning to recognise what you are really being asked is also essential – more about this on Day Five.

You will have been working on the skills for this type of exam throughout your course so far. The ability to make a sound analysis of facts or a situation, to take a viewpoint and argue from it, and to use evidence judiciously to support your argument will already be essential in your course if you are undertaking this type of exam. However, revision can be used to strengthen these abilities even further. If this is the type of exam you face, make sure that you produce as many plans of possible exam essays as you can. This is not because any of those essays will necessarily come up in the exam, but so that you deepen your understanding and perfect your ability to create an effective analysis and a convincing argument.

Blended exams

Some exams ask for a combination of multiple-choice questions, short-answer questions and one or two essays. They require all the skills you will be developing by using this guide, but you will need to be ready to take charge. You might choose to work on the most tiring section first (usually the longer essay) and then move back to the multiple-choice section, to get your brain back up to speed before tackling the short-answer section. As you practise by giving yourself some mock exams, you will find the best way for you – and you can then stick to this in the exam.

Whilst mock exams, plenty of them, will help you develop the skill of switching from one type of exam challenge to another, so too can your other revision tasks. This guide suggests several activities to do each day, and mixing them up frequently on some days, so that you only spend a short amount of time on each task before moving off and then coming back to it, will help train your brain to make that type of switch effectively.

Class tests

These might be in hard copy or online, but they are essentially no different from any other exam, except that you might have shorter notice that they are about to happen. If you know that your course includes class tests, it is a good idea to ask at the outset how often, and when, they might happen.

Success in class tests often relies on your ability to work well under pressure of both time and distractions. An exam room, silent and large, perhaps with strangers beside you, can make it easy to shut yourself off and think; your usual classroom can make this far less easy. It is worth doing some practice tests with your revision group – in the classroom, if this is possible. If not, you can occasionally introduce an artificial distraction (such as music or the television on in the background) whilst you practise.

Peer review

Sometimes all or part of your mark will be made up from assessment of your work by your fellow students. This usually follows a group project or event, such as a presentation or special project. This need not concern you unduly, but it is worth asking about how it will actually work. Is your mark decided solely by your peers, or will the instructor have some say in it? On what grounds are you being assessed? How are the available marks distributed? This type of assessment need not cause you problems, as long as you know how it works.

Learning to criticise the work of a fellow student in a way that is simultaneously positive and meaningful is not easy. During the early stages of the process, ask for feedback on your feedback – this can be done online as part of the peer review if that makes it easier.

Exam strategy

There is no 'right way' to master exam papers, so you have strategic decisions to make based upon these different types of exam, and it makes sense to start thinking about them now:

1 In a multiple-choice test, it can be helpful to answer all of the questions where you feel confident first, and then to go back to the beginning and work through those you left behind. This can work well, but it has the danger of allowing you to dash through so quickly that you make mistakes. If that tends to happen to you, you might prefer to answer the questions in the order in which they are set, so that you can let the test pace your timing for you. A few practice runs through examples of

past papers (or even doing some online quizzes about anything at all) will reveal whether it is safe for you to rush through with your 'easy' answers first.

2 In a short-answer exam the greatest danger is timing: you might give too much time to one answer at the expense of another, or feel under so much time pressure that you do not do justice to your early answers. Use mock exams to help you decide whether this is likely to be a problem for you; if it is, make sure that you put the time when you aim to finish against each plan you make. In an essay exam paper, would you feel most comfortable giving your strongest answer first, or starting with your weakest and moving on from there? Do you prefer to plan all of your answers first, then write out the complete answers, or would you rather take each answer in itself, plan it and write it before you move on?

3 In a blended exam, which section would you prefer to tackle first (multiple-choice, short answers or longer essay)? Use mock exams to find out your answer to this important question.

4 If you are taking class tests, trying out mock exams is often best done in your normal lesson group, so that you familiarise yourself with that situation before you take the test.

Think about these different approaches in your mock exams, or think back to previous exams and what worked for you, and plan your strategy in advance, so that you have the best chance of success in each exam.

Well done! This has been a hard work day, and you have taken the first, important step: you are now organised and ready to move on, safe in the knowledge that you can achieve the best possible result in the time available. These basics are vital, so do not skimp on them: if you have not completed it all today, set aside a little time tomorrow to catch up with yourself.

Exams are not designed as traps to fail you. Your tutors are willing you to succeed, and will have designed the assessment to give you the most help possible. They are simply trying to take a snapshot of where you are now; exams give you the best chance to shine, to show that you are developing in a subject area and are keen to succeed. Such ambition is always rewarded.

What nobody tells you as they teach you is that no student *could* know, or would ever be *expected* to know, 100% of the material on a course. In most cases, you will already know at least 50% of what you need to remember as you begin to revise, and for most courses you only need to aim to know about 70–80% of the material. This is because credit comes from doing more than simply recalling information with no judgement or analysis; it comes from how you *use* your knowledge, and that is what you will be doing from now on.

Things to do today

☐ Yesterday you divided your material into eight sections. You will be working on the first of those today. Reduce the material in your first section by working through it, at a reasonably fast pace, and making revision notes, the briefer the better, ready to make some revision cards later.

☐ Only look up the minimum amount of information, at points where you now realise, looking back on the material, that you have not understood something. Some of your material can be left behind at this point, as you can safely assume that you will not need to use it in the exams.

☐ Take a break. This is an easier day than some – you are only tackling one section of your material – but that is deliberate. You need time to find your best rhythm of working, and to mull over what you have been working on today.

⮕ Smarter learning

You might notice that some of the material you have to leave behind as part of your revision will be useful to you in future courses. Make a note of these points or references in a separate document which you can look through after the exams. That way, you are preparing for the future as you go along.

Testing yourself in the early stages

Later on, you will be able to test your knowledge by planning some practice exam answers. At this stage, you simply need to consider how much you actually know. This comes in part from making notes: be firm with yourself and only write in your revision notes the essentials; as you go through the material, keep on your shoulder a 'know-it gremlin'. That is, if you feel familiar with the facts as you write them out in brief, make a conscious point of noting this to yourself. By the time you have reduced the material to revision notes, you will have a good sense of how much you know already. Keep your know-it gremlin on your shoulder throughout – it will guide you when it comes to later revision.

Give yourself a break once you have produced the revision notes for a section, then go back and be brutal: highlight the sections that you really need, and cross out all of the notes you know so well that you will not have to consider them again, and any notes that you can see now are superfluous to your needs.

Once you have your revision notes in place, you will be ready to reduce them even further by producing revision cards. Making revision cards is an art, and it is one you will need to practise as you move forward. You are aiming to produce small postcard-sized cards, with only essential information on them. This might be a list of facts, or some quotes to remember, or an essay plan, or a series of connections that you have noticed.

As the exam approaches, in the last day or so, you will also make 'last minute' revision cards. There will probably be only one of these for each exam, and they will only include those few facts that you believe you will never be able to remember for longer than a few minutes. As soon as you get into the exam you will jot down these facts on your planning pages, so that you can relax and focus on the task ahead of you.

What is 'essential information'?

It is easy to suggest that you only note down the essential information from your course notes; it can be hard to do this in practice. You will need a light touch with your full notes as you reduce them, and one way to do this is to imagine all of the material as a beach. As you wander across the beach, every now and then you will see a rock sticking up out of the sand – a piece of information or an idea that really sticks out for you. It might be that you remember it vividly from your lessons, or that it is something that helps make sense of an idea for you. In your notes, these rocks are often the short sentences that you noted down to sum up a whole section of a lecture, or the first sentence you wrote as you listened in a classroom.

As you progress you will find it easier to see the rocks standing up from the sand. The trick is to scan your notes, skim-reading sections and all the time asking yourself 'What is the sand that I am leaving behind? Where are the rocks in these notes?'

Memory techniques

Although learning styles will play a part not only in how you learn but also in how you revise, there is no one style that will suit you to the exclusion of the others: we all have a predominant learning style, but we can also benefit from dipping into other ways to learn and recall. This allows you to tap into several types of memory techniques, so that your revision does not become boring. You will want to use your preferred technique most of the time, but trying out all of them might throw up some nice surprises. It may be that you end up using most of them, just to break up your routine, even if you spend the majority of your time favouring one of them.

You may already know your preferred learning style, or the descriptions earlier in this guide will have given you enough clues to be able to make an educated guess at which is your style. You can also use the revision techniques described in the next few pages to test which is your preferred learning style. If you think you are a visual learner, for example, try out the revision method that is suggested here for that type of learner when you first come to revise. If it works well for you, and you seem to be moving forward as you had hoped, that is the method you will use for most of your revising, varying every now and then just for a break in the routine. If you feel less comfortable than you had hoped, look back at the learning style chart and try out another method that you think might suit you … it will not take you long to find your most effective revision method.

A memory technique for visual learners: the method of loci

This is sometimes called building a 'memory room' or a 'mind palace', and it is an ancient way to memorise that still works today.

Imagine a place that you know well – a room, or your whole house, usually works well. Then, as you look at your revision cards, imagine putting each piece of information in a different place in the space. Take your time and really try to see it in your mind's eye, with the pieces of information exactly where you put them. If you have an essay plan you are trying to recall, you could try placing the information in a journey around the location you have chosen, so that when you try to recall the plan, you can imagine yourself walking around the scene, picking up information in the right order.

Top tip: It can take practice to master this way of doing things. If you are a visual learner it should come to you relatively easily, but you might need some determination to persevere in the early stages.

A memory technique for aural learners: mnemonics

You probably already do this from time to time – most of us do – but it is worth developing this technique more fully now that you are focusing on exams. A mnemonic is an easy-to-recall phrase that uses the same initial letters as the facts that you wish to remember: '**R**ichard **o**f **Y**ork **g**ave **b**attle **i**n **v**ain' is a common mnemonic, allowing us to remember the colours of the rainbow in the order in which they appear (**r**ed, **o**range, **y**ellow, **g**reen, **b**lue, **i**ndigo and **v**iolet).

It does not matter how crazy the mnemonic is – if you can recall it, it is the right one for you. You will find yourself becoming attached to some of your mnemonics for years. Some people know the order of points of the compass as 'never eat shredded wheat' and others use 'naughty elephants squirt water': you would struggle to persuade either of these groups to change their mnemonic. As an aural learner you might find this technique even more powerful if you set your mnemonics to music – a little jingle that you make up, or perhaps the chorus of a favourite song.

Top tip: Before you begin work on making up your own mnemonic, ask if there are any already in existence in your subject areas. Mnemonics that become traditional in an area of study are usually those that work well.

A memory technique for verbal learners: record and repeat

In some ways the verbal learner is in a strong position. You can tap into many of the methods described here and simply read the material out loud in order to recall it later. The challenge lies in the fact that reading something aloud once will not be enough to guarantee recall. You probably already realise this, now that you think about the number of times you have tried to persuade family and friends to test you on your notes so that you can hear yourself say the answers out loud repeatedly to help you to remember them.

Having supporters to give you the chance to say what you know so as to aid recall is valuable; if you are a social learner, you are probably very happy in a revision group where you will find talking through the material out loud beneficial. If you are a solitary learner, you could get into the habit of recording (on your phone, perhaps) your revision cards by reading them aloud and then playing the recordings back several times. When you test yourself against your cards, rather than writing down the facts that you remember, try speaking them out loud and then checking the recording against your written cards before you reduce the information on them.

Top tip: If a revision group works well for you as a verbal learner, there is no need to abandon the idea once your exams are over. Think about starting up, or joining, a study group for your next course or module.

A memory technique for kinaesthetic learners: whole-body learning

Sitting still and looking at revision cards can be agony for a kinaesthetic learner, who will need to move in order to function at optimal level. For you, this might be little more than walking around as you recite or read what is on your cards. For some learners, though, it may be much more involved.

You might, for example, make a model to demonstrate to yourself, and so remember, how a process works; or you might cover an entire wall with a huge timeline, one that you have to walk up and down in order to see the detail. If you are trying out the 'memory palace' technique, you would need to actually walk around the room as you practise recalling the items that you have put there; indeed, you might prefer to place physical cards around a physical room with brief notes on them.

If you are in a revision group with several kinaesthetic learners, you might all want to 'act out' a theory or a concept, finding a physical representation with your bodies and movement. Once you have found the right group, with similar views on how to do this, you are likely to work together in the future.

Top tip: Kinaesthetic memory techniques take time and imagination to be successful. If you are short on time, or have mobility issues, you will still always benefit from some level of movement as you revise, even if it is no more than tapping your fingers rhythmically on a desk.

A memory technique for logical learners: systems thinking

For a logical learner, a list of facts with nothing else to support them will be difficult to understand and recall: you might even find yourself losing track of where you are in your revision cards. For you, making a system of facts will resolve this potential problem and also make your recall significantly more powerful. Your revision cards might not be lists of points but might instead be facts written down in order of importance, or with arrows between facts to show patterns, or with colour shaded areas of the cards that correspond to the different effects and implications of the facts. Although you will not want to be too rigid in thinking towards one potential exam answer (the exam itself is going to throw you a different question), you might well feel more comfortable creating 'connections cards' (more on these later) right from the outset, and you might produce these in a plan form such as a spider chart. This might lead to you remembering slightly fewer facts, but you will be fully ready to use them whatever the exam question.

Top tip: Because you recall so well in this way if you are a logical learner, it is worth spending some time with your first few revision cards, seeing what 'system builders' help you most, such as tables, flowcharts, spider charts, colours or symbols.

In addition to any of the memory techniques above, you will also want to keep in mind whether you tend to be a social or a solitary learner, as this will influence whether you want to use these techniques in a group or not.

⇒ Smarter learning

In sharing all of these memory techniques the emphasis has been on remembering information, but the benefit of finding the right technique is far greater than this. Once you have decided which of them suit you best, you will use them as you learn. Perhaps your lecture or lab notes will look different in future, matching more to one of these techniques. In ordering information for an assignment, you might use your preferred method, either as you think it through or as you plan it on paper. By mastering these techniques now, you are guaranteeing yourself a longer-term gain.

Before you look at the next few pages, think about everything you have ever heard (or learnt) about Shakespeare's play *Romeo and Juliet*. Then read on to see how revision cards work …

Revision cards: how they might look

Imagine that you are revising for an exam about Shakespeare's play *Romeo and Juliet*. Here are examples of cards you might need to make – note that every card has a title so that you can glance at it in the future and test yourself.

Revision card: an example of a basic card

Romeo and Juliet: facts

- *Romeo and Juliet* written (probably) in 1594 or 1595.
- Already a well-known story – from Arthur Brooke's poem (1562).
- It has a prologue, like Greek chorus – in sonnet form.
- Montague and Capulet – the two families – reconciled in the end.
- Imaginative language and comic relief used.
- Luhrmann's film (1996) – modern take on the play with original language.

Revision card: an example of a connections card

You would need to know several of Shakespeare's plays to make these particular connections, but connections like these will be clear to you from your own course.

> ### Romeo and Juliet: connections
>
> - Typical tragedy – reconciliation at the end – like *King Lear*.
> - Young lovers being wayward – like *A Midsummer Night's Dream*.
> - Jealous love leading to death – like *Othello*.
> - Young girl dying – like *Othello* and *King Lear*.
> - Idea of fate controlling events – like *Macbeth*.
> - Young man struggling with his destiny – like *Hamlet*, perhaps?

Revision card: an example of an essay plan card

> Essay topic: Is Luhrmann's 1996 film *Romeo + Juliet* effective in reaching a teenage audience?

Yes, because:
→ the main characters are young
→ it is romantic, and tragic
→ a modern film adaptation makes it accessible
→ it covers issues that are still relevant today.

No, because:
→ maybe the lovers are too young to be acceptable?
→ religion and fate are invoked – too complicated?
→ the language is challenging – would this be a barrier?

Revision card: an example of a 'last minute' card

This card is not attempting to capture a whole course; it is a way to remember, just before you go into an exam, the random facts that you know you keep forgetting.

- Arthur Brooke – 1562
- Written 1594/5
- Romeo's best friend – Mercutio
- Modern film – *Romeo + Juliet* – Baz Luhrmann, 1996

Information-gathering and sorting software and apps

You might also already be using, or are considering using, electronic note organisation apps, such as Endnote or Evernote. These can do a fantastic job of helping you to search material easily (even handwritten notes) and to use your notes in a far more active way. You can add links easily, organise your material under tabs, have notes created from voice notes and quickly see how one area of work might relate to another. You can annotate screen clips, import sources and merge notes. If you like visual prompts as you learn and recall, these apps can offer you those as well.

This all sounds perfect – and it can be. But *only* if it works well for you. For many students, using this type of app becomes part of their everyday study life and makes it far easier for them to power through revision. For others, it takes up too much of their time, or leaves them with beautifully organised material that is actually many times more than the material that they need to learn well and revise successfully.

⬤➡ Smarter learning

Apps are another way you can use your revision time to work towards your long-term learning goals. You could start using these apps whilst you revise, perhaps in a limited way if you do not have much time, and then extend your use of them to support your learning in a much more profound way when you move back into the lecture hall or classroom.

Getting to know your 'know-it gremlin'

Gremlins are usually thought of as mythical little creatures which mischievously make things go wrong. Your know-it gremlin is quite different, and can be your greatest ally in revising. It will help you to be confident. Imagine this little creature sitting on your shoulder, whispering in your ear 'You know it!' Your gremlin will do this when you test yourself on a detailed revision card and are ready to reduce it to a much briefer card. It will do it again to give you the confidence to set aside a card once you know it. And when you come to practice exams it will be there too, whispering in your ear as you produce the best possible plan.

You will know when you are ignoring your gremlin, either because you are rereading a card over and over again with no real sense of how much you know, or because you are panicking and going back to material you mastered days ago.

We all have a know-it gremlin. Yours is whispering to you when you suddenly find yourself relaxing, relieved that you have lodged something soundly in your brain. If you can learn to recognise how this feels, you are firmly on the road to success.

Day 3

Things to do today

❑ Reduce your revision notes for Section One of your material to revision cards. Be bold: only include the essentials on each revision card, with your 'know-it gremlin' firmly on your shoulder.

❑ Reduce Section Two of your material to revision notes.

You are now into the swing of revision: sifting through the material you have, pulling out the important information and making revision notes, leaving them overnight and then reducing them onto revision cards. You will carry this process on right up until Day Eleven, and it will be at the core of your revision. Almost without realising it is happening, you will be learning as you go and remembering as you write, so that you can emerge at the end with the information you need to succeed.

The rhythm of your revision

It is simply not possible to work at 100% efficiency for hours and hours on end. All of us need to take a rest at times, and you will need to learn how you work best.

The easiest way to discover your best working rhythm is to time yourself: check how many pages of material you reduce into revision notes in the first 20 minutes of your revision session today, and then the second 20 minutes, and so on. You will find that at some point your work rate drops dramatically. This will vary from person to person, but when you have pinpointed the 'drop point' for you, you will know when to take a break. As you revise more, you may well be able to work efficiently for longer, so check yourself in this way every couple of days.

'Taking a break' here might be just that: a drink, a walk about, maybe a snack and a complete rest from work for some time. If this is what you need, then take this type of break. A word of warning, though: try to avoid doing things in the break that will lead you too far away from revision. Checking a few emails, with a time limit, might be useful; logging on to social media and finding that an hour has gone by is far less useful! You need to be ready to return to your revision as soon as your brain has cleared and you feel less tired.

Of course, taking a break might not mean having to leave revision behind. It can be equally beneficial (and more productive) to simply change your task. If you are working on revision cards, then go back to making revision notes for the next section, or, in the later stages, produce a few essay plans.

Be true to yourself

Some people are naturally very methodical, planning each challenge in detail and working through the tasks in a regular way. By the time they reach an exam, they have spent weeks, maybe months, familiarising themselves with the material. Others take a last-minute approach, cramming for exams in the last few days, or hours, and relying on flair and adrenaline to get them through.

Both of these approaches can work: methodical workers have the reassurance that they are progressing smoothly, but can get bored with the material and struggle to retain all of the information; last-minute workers have to hope they are not struck down with flu, and are more likely to miss vital information.

You can improve your performance. If you are methodical, varying your tasks regularly will reduce the dangers of boredom; if you are a last-minute worker, the rigid structure of this guide will keep you motivated. However, whichever type of student you are, there is very little point in trying to be other than you are. The way of working that has seen you through life so far will carry on working for you, because it is what suits you.

Taking stock

You have now achieved the most important part of your revision. You have got to grips with the process and are well on your way to achieving the ultimate goal: succeeding in the exam.

I know how my exams will look ☑

I know where they all are ☑

I have divided all of my material ☑

I can pace myself ☑

I can reduce my notes ☑

I have made my revision cards ☑

I can see how course work and exams work ☑

I recognise my 'know it' gremlin ☑

Things to do today

❑ Reduce your revision notes for Section Two of your material to revision cards.

❑ Reduce Section Three of your material to revision notes.

By now you will be getting into the rhythm of your revising. Each day will include repetitious tasks, but what makes it interesting is that the material is different from day to day. Some days will be quite easy if you already feel comfortable with the material; other days will be more challenging. By overlapping material, as you begin to work it up into plans and structures and, later, into further reduced cards, you will be refreshing your memory and working the material as you press on ahead.

On the days when you feel less familiar with the material, you might need to refer to some secondary material to make things clear to you, and this can bring with it benefits and dangers …

Secondary sources

These should be used very sparingly during your revision. You have your notes and handouts from your course: going to other sources, such as books, journals and the internet, can be a huge and distracting time waster.

If you realise that you absolutely need to check out an area (if, for example, your notes are unclear or you know you did not really understand the topic in the first place), try following these guidelines for texts:

▶ Know before you go to the library or resource centre exactly *what* you need to look at and *why* you are looking at it. You must identify beforehand the gaps in your knowledge that you are trying to fill.

▶ You do not have to go to a library or resource centre to look at the internet, but some students prefer the discipline of doing all of their research in one place. It can help to avoid time wasting, so decide in advance whether this could work for you.

▶ Make a list of sources to look at and stick to it – no wandering the aisles or the internet in search of inspiration!

▶ Use the index and table of contents of each book or journal to give you a sense of how much it might help you and as quick guides to its contents.

- Make sure that the book or journal is up to date enough for your purposes.

- Your library should be able to offer you most material in electronic format, so try this first if you find it easier to skim through on a screen rather than in hard copy.

- Photocopy or print out only the pages you really need and then use them as if they were your condensed notes (reducing them to revision cards), but skim-read them first before you make the commitment to photocopy or print them: do you really need them?

- Use your librarians! They are the absolute experts in managing material and will save you hours of time, as well as showing you how to find the perfect resource.

⟶ Smarter learning

It is one thing to decide in advance only to print or copy the material you really need – it is quite another thing to being able to avoid the temptation to print or copy just a few more pages of information here and there, until you have an unexpectedly large pile of unnecessary material to wade through. One way to reduce your stress would be to have a separate area in your study space (either on your computer or in a physical file) where you can hide away material that you find interesting but that you know is not really needed for your revision. That way, you will have something to review after the exams, as you prepare for your next course. You will also have the satisfaction of knowing that your revision time has been well spent in preparing you not just for your exams, but also for your future learning.

Secondary sources: the internet

The internet is the single most alluring time waster known to students, so be very careful as you use it during revision. Try following these guidelines for the internet:

- Be focused: any search engine will bring up too many site options, so be ruthless in honing in on what you need.
- Ask your tutors to recommend specific sections of particular sites.
- Make a 'shopping list' in advance of your search, so you know where you are going to look.
- Only print off the pages you are sure you need, and use them just as you would your lecture or revision notes.
- Do not file the pages until you have pulled them apart and reduced them to brief revision cards; otherwise, they may lurk and distract you.
- Set yourself a strict time limit for online revision activities and stick to it.
- Keep your know-it gremlin on your shoulder at all times – there is no point in printing off material you already know.
- Never assume that, because a source is online, it is up to date. With printed texts and internet material, always check the date when it was released.

Just how much do you need to know?

The quick answer is: probably not nearly as much as you think you need to know. If exams are all about how you *use* your knowledge, then the most important task in your revision will not be cramming more and more material into your head, but using the material and grasping concepts so that you are deepening your understanding and are in the best position to analyse what you have, and how to use it.

From Day Six, I will be encouraging you to produce essay and exam plans. These will stop you from getting bored, as they use your knowledge, and they will give you a much clearer idea of what you know and – more importantly – what you actually need to know.

One way to decide whether you need to approach secondary sources is to produce a quick brainstorm of the important points from your notes. Just capture the ideas and facts as you find them and then take a look – do you have enough material already?

This technique is also useful when you want to test your recall of an area. Use the same method, but do not refer to your notes at all. This will not give you as complete a picture as a more detailed plan, but it is quick and can be reassuring.

Here is an example of a brainstorm on a topic. There are not many facts, but there are ideas that are essential for grasping the bigger picture:

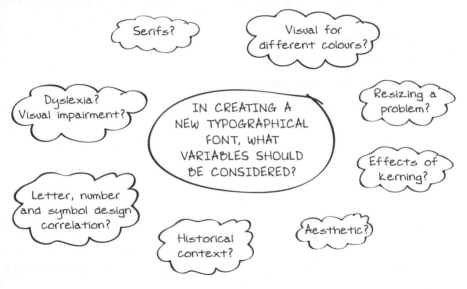

Serifs?

Visual for different colours?

Dyslexia? Visual impairment?

IN CREATING A NEW TYPOGRAPHICAL FONT, WHAT VARIABLES SHOULD BE CONSIDERED?

Resizing a problem?

Effects of kerning?

Letter, number and symbol design correlation?

Historical context?

Aesthetic?

Things to do today

❑ Reduce your revision notes for Section Three of your material to revision cards.

❑ Reduce Section Four of your material to revision notes.

From now on you are going to be working on further reductions. Your revision cards will not stay as they are: you will need to be more active in how you use them. There is no set pattern for this, but each day take the time to test yourself on a batch of your cards (you do not need to divide them into each section's cards for this; just test yourself on as many as you can in the time you have available).

Be confident about what you know: when you have a few spare minutes, pick up some of the cards, check the title of the card, cover it up and try to recite or write down as much as you can remember. Once you have done this three or four times and feel that you know most of what is on some of the cards, you can reduce them still further by rewriting them more compactly and taking out any extraneous material, and use fewer cards for each section of material.

Below is an example showing three revision cards on the topic of book covers and the impact they have on a reader. The fourth card shows how the first three might be reduced once you have tested yourself on them three or four times:

- Colour might attract a casual browser in a bookshop.
- Black and white can also be intriguing and draw a reader in.
- In bookshops, most books are displayed showing their spines, so the spine has to work hard.
- For an e-book, the cover features might have far less impact.
- Awards can be important, especially with second or third editions.

- Awards are often prominently displayed on book covers, sometimes with a gold embossed logo.
- Endorsements by leading newspapers or other authors can also help to sell a book, as can endorsements by celebrities or recommendations on TV shows.
- All this only works if a reader respects the awards or celebrity or likes the TV show!!

- Images are important, especially for 'holiday reads' that might be 'impulse buys' on a journey.
- A good cover image can tell the reader something of the genre of the book and the readership it is trying to capture.
- Stock images are sometimes used on book covers, and this can be disappointing for the reader as they detract from a book's individuality.
- Readers may feel betrayed if the cover does not match the book's content.

Here is an example of a reduced revision card for these three, after successful memorising:

- Physical books differ from e-books.
- Colour vs B/W – remember spines.
- Endorsements and awards – good but can be risky.
- Images – impulse buy, genre clear, BUT stock images or misleading covers break trust.

From now on, you would put the first three cards away and only revise from this final card. These headings should prompt you to recall the full set of information in that area. If that does not happen, look back to your other cards for a moment to check the detail. You will do this less and less as time goes on. When you are confident about knowing the reduced card, put it firmly to one side. As the pile of cards gets smaller, you will know that you are making progress!

⮕ Smarter learning

Note how the student has realised that a minor point about e-books and hard-copy books now heads the revision card. Revision is always about learning as well as remembering, and making decisions about what is most important will help you as you progress.

Essay exams: what the questions mean …

The first thing to work out is what an essay title is actually asking you to do: the words used in the title are crucial. Only after that do you think about planning, which we will cover tomorrow. Here are some of the most **common keywords** used in essay titles:

Keyword	What you are expected to do
Compare	Highlight similarities (and perhaps differences) and, sometimes, offer a preference for one option or another.
Contrast	Bring out the differences between two topics, or two aspects of a topic.
Discuss/Consider	This is the widest possible instruction: you will be considering several aspects of the topic, and perhaps developing an argument.
Examine	This is generally a little easier. You are being asked to look in detail at the topic, but will not necessarily be expected to develop an argument.
Explore	This is similar to 'examine', except that you will range more widely, but still in great detail.
Describe	This is very specific, and you must follow the detail in the title carefully to make sure that you only describe what is relevant.

Keyword	What you are expected to do
State	This is usually used for briefer essays, where you will be describing something (usually a series of facts) but in a less extended way than if you were asked to 'describe'.
Analyse	This requires you to divide a subject up and look at each part of the topic in an analytical way. This is often used to evaluate several options given in the title.
Explain	This is similar to 'analyse', but usually with a sense that you are looking at one process or area of a topic, rather than dividing it up into many aspects.
Trace	This is often used for factual essays, where you are describing something, aiming to explain how something has developed.
Outline	This is similar to 'trace', except that you are usually covering a broader topic. You are being asked to make general points about an area.
Summarise	Here you are being asked to bring a subject under control, to show your understanding of the topic by being able to put forward its key points briefly.
Evaluate	This one is tricky: rather than being tempted to describe the topic, you are expected to use your knowledge to make a judgement about a topic or to give an opinion.

Six ways to feel good

Everyone needs encouragement when they are revising. Here are six ways to make yourself feel better if your enthusiasm starts to dip:

1 Brainstorm an area you have not revised yet. It will remind you of how much you already know and boost your confidence.
2 Do something else. Take half an hour to remind yourself that there is a world beyond your revision.
3 Make a firm date to do something relaxing and/or exciting a few days after your exams finish.
4 Make a 'happy pot'. Write notes to yourself, or jot down inspirational quotes, fold them and keep them in a pot, so that you can dip in and be inspired whenever you need it.
5 If you live with friends, make a shared happy pot for you all, with encouraging notes to each other.
6 Keep in touch by email with a friend who is not studying your subject, so that you cannot bog each other down in the detail – you can email from time to time if you need an encouraging word.

Things to do today

❏ Reduce your revision notes for Section Four of your material to revision cards.

❏ Reduce Section Five of your material to revision notes.

❏ Reduce your pile of revision cards (as many as you have time to do). You will do some of these each day, so that you gradually see the pile reducing.

❏ Begin working on exam plans.

There are two ways to reduce your pile of revision cards: you could follow the guide on Day Five, so that you end up with far fewer cards, or, if you feel more confident in an area, you could go straight to making a detailed essay plan for that area. At this stage, you could just brainstorm a topic. If you find that you have left very little out, all of the topic cards can be discarded and you can revise from your plan or brainstorm.

Essay planning

It is far easier to remember things if you are using your knowledge, and essay plans are a good way to do this. Even if most of your exams are multiple-choice or short-answer exams, planning can help you to use, and therefore more easily recall, the material you need. You will come to know the best method for you as you practise. Over the next few pages there are examples of how different methods might be used.

Planning essays at this stage can feel strange: why do this when you are not going to be given the same question in the exam? It is useful because it helps you see how you could use information for several purposes and in different ways, so that you are ready, regardless of the question. This is especially the case if some of your exams are short-answer exams. By making plans for both short-answer exams and full-length exam essays, you will get a good feel for the differences between those two experiences. This will prepare you well for making the most of your knowledge in those two settings.

Creating a brainstorm

A brainstorm is not a complete planning method in itself; it is a way to help your brain to produce a series of good ideas.

- In the centre of the page, put the central idea (this could be a few key words from the essay title or area of discussion).

- Around the page, and in no particular order, jot down other thoughts that arise from that one central idea. You can be as wide-ranging as you like, and not every idea has to be perfect: often irrelevant ideas might be abandoned later, but will have helped you initially by pushing your mind towards other areas of thought.

- Once you feel that you have drained your brain of all the ideas you might want to cover, be firm and cross out any ideas/thoughts/facts that, on reflection, would not help you in an exam. Go back to the idea of rocks on the beach: what is the necessary information for this particular exam answer – what will support your analysis and argument most effectively?

Brainstorm example

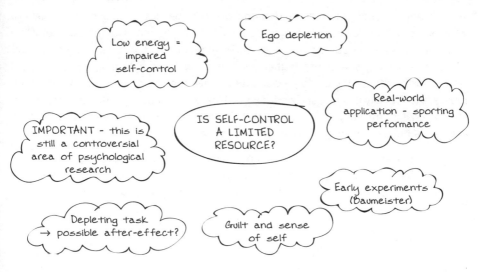

Low energy = impaired self-control

Ego depletion

IMPORTANT - this is still a controversial area of psychological research

IS SELF-CONTROL A LIMITED RESOURCE?

Real-world application - sporting performance

Depleting task → possible after-effect?

Guilt and sense of self

Early experiments (Baumeister)

Using a brainstorm

You are now left with good, solid ideas on which to base a fuller plan. They will not be in any order, or developed to any great extent, so you may like to use one of the other methods described here to make a fuller, more detailed plan from which to write. If you have any doubts about whether you are left with the right material, or you feel worried at this stage, you could produce four or five brainstorms in a row, for different topic areas. Usually this anxiety is caused by lack of familiarity with the process. If you still feel unsure, try working in a group so that you can gain a consensus view, or take a series of brainstorms to your lecturer for comment.

Some students always rely on a brainstorm as the first stage in essay planning; others use them far more sparingly. How often you use them will depend on how well they suit the way your mind works, so practising a few will give you a sense of whether they will be helpful to you.

The best use of a brainstorm in an exam is to reduce your anxiety, as they let you put many ideas on paper quickly, so that your brain is less clogged with facts that you fear you might forget. They are also useful in those cases where you are sure you know about 90% of what is being asked of you, but you have a niggling feeling that you are missing something: a brainstorm will help it to surface. You will not write the answer from the brainstorm, but you will use the information in it to help create your more structured plan.

⮞ Smarter learning

Online brainstorming can be a good way to deepen your learning as you revise. You will be using your existing knowledge to make a brainstorm as it is outlined here, but you could then share your brainstorm by email with a group of your fellow students and ask for their thoughts. At the least, you will then have a larger brainstorm with more ideas ready for the exam. Be firm here: make a note now of those ideas and suggestions that you think will help you in the exams. Put the rest aside, but make sure that you return to them after the exams to see if they could be useful for your next learning challenge.

Creating a spider chart

▶ As with the brainstorm, put your central idea in a circle in the middle of the page.

▶ In circles ranged around the central idea, and joined to it by connecting lines, place the ideas (usually no more than six or so for an exam) that naturally arise from this central point. These are the 'feet' of the 'spider'.

▶ From these 'feet', make more circles and place all of the subsidiary ideas that arise from each of your main points.

▶ Once you have a group of ideas set out in this way, you will be able to add more facts to each area of the spider chart, so that it is as detailed as you need it to be before you start to write.

▶ This type of plan is sometimes called a 'bubble chart'.

Spider chart example

Using a spider chart

For most students the diagram given above is complicated enough, although some students make them far more complicated than this, with arrows showing the order of things and how the ideas connect. Practice will show you how complicated you feel comfortable making your spider charts.

Spider charts are useful if you are being asked to create an argument in an essay: they allow you to range freely without ever losing your way.

Creating a flowchart

▶ Your central idea in a flowchart comes in the first box and is followed by your next idea, in the next box, linked to the first by an arrow.

▶ You can put subsidiary ideas or facts in the boxes below each of these main boxes, again joined by an arrow.

▶ You will not expect to record vastly different ideas or facts between a spider chart and a flowchart; the difference lies in the way those ideas are laid out and the effect this has on your thinking process.

▶ Once your flowchart is complete, you will have a linear set of ideas, set out in a logical flow of thought. It is this linear progression that is the key to flowcharts: it tends to encourage you to write quite fast and with confidence once the chart is complete.

Flowchart example

Analyse how the activities of earthworms in soil can affect the greenhouse gas balance.

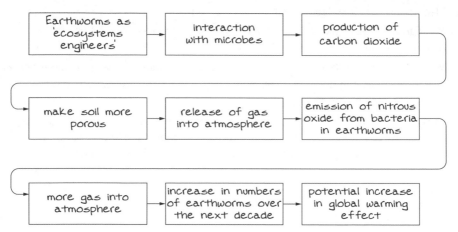

Using a flowchart

Flowcharts are especially useful if you are being asked to describe a process or to show how facts fit together to make a logical picture.

They are also valuable in short-essay answers if you are not being asked to create a complex argument, but instead are simply expected to give a series of facts and ideas.

They also work well if you tend to worry in exams that you might have missed something out. Because each idea flows from the one before it, and is linked to the one after it, it is easy to see at a glance if you have left out a key fact, idea or part of the process.

Creating a mind map

▶ A mind map will be as individual as the person creating it, and there are very few rules to follow. In general, your main idea will still sit centrally in the page, and your subsidiary ideas will come away from that idea.

▶ At each point where you record an idea – so at each section of the mind map – try to use at least three different colours: this helps you to remember more easily what you have written or drawn. In revision this is obviously useful, but it also helps you in an exam, where a quick glance at your mind map will imprint the ideas on your brain.

▶ In the example I have given below there are words and illustrations. Usually these are connected by lines, but you need not include any words if you find it easier to use just pictures, and you could use symbols to connect ideas if you find that clearer than using lines. As with all of these methods, practice will help to show you what works best for you and give you the chance to develop a method to suit your way of working.

Mind map example

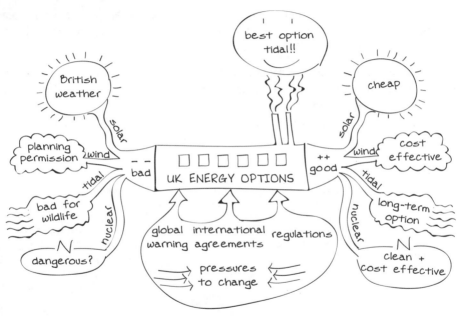

Using a mind map

A mind map can be slower to produce than either a spider chart or a flowchart, but you are less likely to change your mind as you go along, so overall making a mind map need not slow you down in an exam.

Mind maps are useful, of course, for planning essays, and so you will use them in your revision and in the exam. However, spider charts and flowcharts are usually quicker to produce, so you might tend to use these as your main methods for making speedy answer plans as you revise. The greatest advantage of mind maps is that they really do help you to remember complicated series of facts and ideas.

⇒ Smarter learning

One of the many advantages of revision is that you are able to work your material. That is, you sift through it to produce your revision notes, then rework it to make effective revision cards, and then put it to use by making plans. This not only helps you to understand your material more deeply, but also gives you the chance to learn which planning method works best for you. This will help you with exams, and also in all your future learning.

Changing your mind

Spider charts and flowcharts are intended to help you to test your ideas, and to see how they might fit together, along with the facts, to make a whole. In some cases, it is also useful to create one main chart, and then a series of smaller charts to show the detail of some of the more challenging sections of an area.

It is always going to be good to keep an open mind, to be prepared to change your mind as you go along. As you look over your plan and ponder whether it would work as an exam answer, ask yourself these questions:

▶ Can you identify from the plan the most important points that you absolutely have to make?

▶ Does your plan show you the best order in which to make your points?

▶ If you are making an argument, will this plan keep you on track – can you see your way clearly through the whole argument?

▶ Have you included enough, or too much, material to support the points you want to make?

- Will you be able to turn this plan into an answer in the time you are given in the exam, or do you need to cut it down or add to it?

- If you glance back through the revision cards and connection cards for this area, are you still content with the plan?

Later on in your revision, go back to your earlier plans again and consider whether you would change them now that your revision tasks have given you a deeper understanding of the area. What would you do differently now? What would you add, or remove? Would you change the structure of your plan so as to strengthen your answer?

Your know-it gremlin will help you here: if at any point you look at a plan and are pleased with its shape and detail, your gremlin will be whispering in your ear again, saying 'Well done – you know it!'

In revision, you can change your mind as often as you like, and this is all to the good, as it shows that you are developing your ideas and incorporating new facts and theories into your overall view. In an exam you do not have time to keep on changing your mind, but it is still important to be open to the possibility of change and to be prepared to cross out a plan and start again if you really feel that it is not going to work. The few minutes spent on creating a new plan will save you far more time as you write your answer.

The dangers of list plans

Many of us (myself included) enjoy making list plans: simply jotting down a series of headings and sub-headings and adding a few bullet points beneath each to flesh out the ideas.

This method has its benefits – it is quick and usually produces a neat, logical plan – but it also carries the danger of missing out material that needs to be there. List plans have their place. If you feel confident that you have all of the material at your fingertips, they can work well. If you are producing a complex or lengthy answer, or have any doubts about how to arrange your material, it is a good insurance policy to use one of the other methods listed here, just to ensure that nothing is left out. If you find it easier to write from a list plan, it will take only a few moments to convert a diagram plan to a list, and then you can work from it with confidence.

⟶ Smarter learning

You might use any of these planning methods on your revision cards, perhaps as you reduce and rework them in line with your preferred learning style. In the long term, you could try using them as a way to encapsulate complicated material on a single page, so that you can be reminded of a lecture, seminar or series of learning events at a glance. By controlling your material in this way as you go through a course, you will inevitably increase your understanding of a topic.

Timed essay plans

At first, you will probably want to practise essay planning with no time restrictions, so that you get to know which planning methods suit you best. To find out how well you can use your material, untimed essay plans will always serve you well, but you might also want to practise some *timed* essay plans, to get you ready for the exam. I will go through exam timing with you more fully on Day Thirteen, but at this stage we can focus on the planning.

Take *10 minutes* for each essay plan and divide your time:

1 minute to look at the question carefully, to make sure you have grasped all of its implications.

2 minutes to make a six-point list of the key points you want to make.

5 minutes to work this list up into a full plan, using whichever method you prefer.

2 minutes to add any extra detail that comes to you once the plan is complete – dates, quotes, names, extra facts or theories.

Finally, check back to the question: do you think you have answered it fully enough?

What about revision groups?

Revising can leave you feeling isolated, especially if you are a social learner, which is not good for your morale. It is worth considering a group as a source of support.

If you *do* become involved in a revision group, ask yourself these questions:

1 How much time do you have to spend meeting with the group?
2 When you leave, do you feel that it was time well spent?
3 Is the group boosting your confidence, or getting you down?
4 Is the group revising together in a way that suits you?

If your answers show up a problem, you might want to abandon the idea altogether, or you could consider setting up an online revision group, which you can dip in and out of when you have a little free time.

However, you may find that it is becoming a social group, and you cannot resist checking what everyone in the group is saying and doing online, even though you planned to do something else that you know would be more constructive. One way to overcome this is to tell the group when you plan to be online. That way nobody will expect you to be revising online at other times.

Taking stock

You have worked through the first stages of your revision – well done! Now your revision has become far more active – brainstorming, making essay plans and reducing your revision cards. All of this activity will help to keep you motivated.

Things to do today

❑ Rest.

❑ Rest.

❑ Rest.

I know it sounds too good to be true, but it is essential that you take some time out to rest. Your brain needs a break and time to assimilate the material that you have been revising. Even if you feel you are behind in your revision tasks, try to force yourself into a day off – you really do need it.

For some people this means a day of doing nothing much at all, but for most of us it is better to plan a rest day in advance, so that you make the most of it and reduce your stress levels.

Planning a rest day

If you prefer a more structured rest day, try these out:

1 The night before, plan what you hope to achieve in the day (*not* revision tasks!).

2 Do not get up early – even an extra half-hour in bed will feel like a treat.

3 Work through all of the tasks on your list in the morning – this way you will reduce the pressure of life when you get back to revision, but you've given yourself a time limit of just a few hours.

4 Relax completely however you prefer – a nice lunch, a walk, a long bath, watching daytime TV. You will be amazed at how often great thoughts pop into your mind when you are doing nothing.

5 Have a note pad ready to jot down any stray thoughts to do with revision. Note them, and then forget them for the rest of the day.

6 If you have been limiting the amount of time you spend online so that you can get your revision done, perhaps giving yourself just a certain time of day to go online, it is a good idea to stick to the same routine on your rest day. A day trying to 'catch up online' can be exhausting and so leave you with a much less refreshing rest day than you need.

7 Try to spend the afternoon/evening socialising with family or friends, and ask everyone to avoid mentioning revision unless you bring it up – this is the time to forget about it completely.

8 Ideally, get a reasonably early night.

Six more ways to feel good

A rest day will always be beneficial; it is getting back to the revision that can be a problem. You have broken the rhythm of your work, and revising can feel like a real slog after your rest day. Here is how to get over the hurdle:

1 Make a list of the order of your tasks on your first day back.
2 By now, the variety of revision tasks is increasing, so produce a timetable for the day, showing when you are going to do different types of tasks, and include as much variety as you can.
3 If you do not bounce back easily, do not be too hard on yourself – congratulate yourself for every task you conquer.
4 If you do not complete every task, focus at the end of the day on what you have achieved – you will catch up with yourself on the following day as long as you do not lose heart.
5 Reduce the amount of time you usually spend on each task before you move on to another type of revision task.
6 Be prepared to have a longer revision day with far more breaks in it. You will achieve the same amount as normal, but without too much stress.

Things to do today

❑ Reduce your revision notes for Section Five of your material to revision cards.

❑ Reduce Section Six of your material to revision notes.

❑ Keep reducing your pile of revision cards (as many as you have time to do).

❑ Keep going with some general essay plans.

❑ Begin working on past papers or sample assessments.

General essay plans will always be useful, but by now you could also gain from looking at past papers and sample assessments to give yourself some practice with the real thing.

Using past papers

Get hold of as many exam papers as you can: these might be past papers or examples given to you by your tutor. You might also find past papers from similar courses to yours on websites. You have already looked at some past papers on Day One, to get a sense of where you are going. Now you need to work through them with revision in mind:

▶ There is no need to time yourself: just work through and answer the questions as well as you can, and then note where you need to go back and do more work.

▶ There is also no need to produce very detailed answers – just a list of the points you would include, or an essay plan, will be enough to guide you.

▶ Try not to get anxious about producing the perfect answer; instead, work through a whole paper at a time, then go back and decide where your weaknesses (if any) lie.

▶ Be bold: assess the paper in its entirety, and only make a note of areas where you are absolutely sure you need to do more work.

▶ For these areas, pull out the fuller revision cards that you discarded earlier (and, if you really need to, your notes on these areas), and spend time rereading and testing yourself.

▶ As soon as you feel confident, discard the cards and only pick them up again if that area trips you up later in a practice answer.

In some institutions, those who set the exams are required to produce some general feedback about how students answered a paper; sometimes this feedback is given for each question. If you take a look at previous feedback on the exams you are about to take, you might gain some inside information about how to do well, but be careful. If there is a significant problem with how past students tackled a particular question, and so there is plenty of feedback on it, the examiner may well have decided not to include a question like that in future. It could be that it did not reflect the learning on a course well enough, and so it will not be set again. When you are looking at any feedback of this sort, remember that there is no guarantee that similar questions will be set in the future.

⫘➤ Smarter learning

When you are considering your next course, looking at past papers and the feedback on them can offer you some valuable pointers on how to approach the course.

The art of procrastination

'Procrastination' is our ability to be very busy doing nothing much, and we often become experts in this during revision time. At the end of a day's revision, many of us find our books ordered alphabetically on the shelf, our emails sorted into files, our pets (or even our neighbour's pets) walked for several miles and our distant friends and relatives delighted by our unexpected phone call. We also find that the 'To do' revision list for the day has not really dwindled much at all.

We all need to procrastinate a bit – we are not learning machines, after all, and procrastination can be a positive force in revision. As you procrastinate, your mind ticks over with all of the things you have learnt recently, and you find that you go back to revision knowing more than you thought. This is why those who enjoy computer games or are learning to play the piano are often amazed at how they improve once they have left it alone for a day.

So, a *little* procrastination is good, but you must be vigilant …

Anti-procrastination checklist

- Decide in advance when you are going to take breaks, and stick to your plan.
- Turn off your mobile when you are trying to focus on a task.
- Never 'nip onto' a social network site – you can lose an hour before you even notice.
- Try using the same procrastination task every time you need a break – this might be doing a huge pile of washing, or answering three emails in each break (but no more), or texting six friends (and then turning your mobile off again). The rhythm will help to keep you on track.
- If you find yourself looking out of the window far too much, or rereading the same revision card several times, take a proper break and allow yourself a set amount of time before you try again.
- Vary your tasks – always. This helps to keep you interested in what you are doing.
- Save some 'easy tasks' for each day, so that you can lower the pressure whilst still getting through the work.
- We all work poorly on low blood sugar or when dehydrated, so have a snack and a drink beside you to keep you going.
- If you are losing your way, a brainstorm of the area you are working on can help bring you back on track.

Day 9

Things to do today

□ Reduce your revision notes for Section Six of your material to revision cards.

□ Reduce Section Seven of your material to revision notes.

□ Keep reducing your pile of revision cards (as many as you have time to do).

□ Go back to past essays for inspiration.

So far, you have been focusing on gathering and remembering information and putting it to use. Today, take some time to read a few of the assignments you have produced during your course. This is a good way to remind yourself of how you have used information in the past, and could inspire you as you remember all the good work that you have done already.

When you find an assignment you did that covers material likely to come up in the exam, try making a spider chart or mind map of it on a revision card, so that you can remember exactly how you did it.

How to tackle a seen exam and an open book exam

There are two ways in which your tutors might try to help you: by giving you an exam paper in advance, so that you can prepare your answer thoroughly before the exam (a 'seen exam'), and by letting you take key texts into the exam (an 'open book exam'). Both of these situations bring dangers with them.

For a seen exam, writing out the whole answer and trying to memorise it can cause problems – if you lose your place in the exam and cannot remember your prepared answer exactly, you run the risk of missing out whole sections and panicking. Instead, write a good opening and closing and leave the rest in plan form, so that you know the material but are not tied to the words. You will need your know-it gremlin close at hand for this part, to reassure you that a plan is sufficient and that you will know what to write in the exam because you know the material behind the plan.

You are already making essay plans as part of your revision, so this need be no different, except that you will be adding more detail than usual and you will have your books and notes to guide you as you make the plan.

For the seen exam question 'Discuss the advances in state education during the late nineteenth century', you could produce something like this for your opening paragraph:

> *Various forms of education were already in place by the late nineteenth century. Dame Schools, workers' education programmes and fee-paying grammar schools all existed. The Victorian Age was one of advancement, and education took its place in that march of progress.*

This opening shows that you have a good overall grasp of the subject area. It also gives an indication of the historical approach you intend to take, acting as a springboard to the body of your answer. The spider chart on the next page shows how you might structure the remainder of the essay.

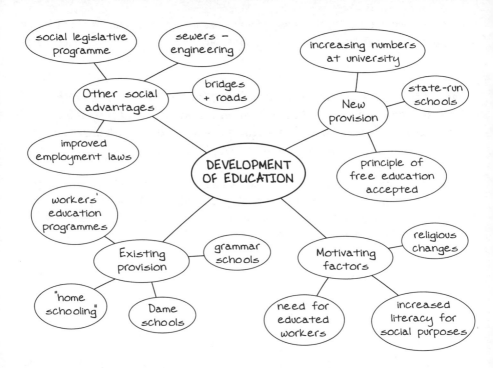

Your closing section must also be strong and may include a paragraph reiterating the main points you have made. The final sentence must be firm and show your overview of the topic. The closing to this essay could be something like this:

> *Today we still reap the benefits of Victorian progress. Many of the sewers under our big cities are Victorian and so are some of our major bridges. However, unlike these successful and long-lasting structures upon which we rely every day, state education still has some way to go before it can fulfil the dreams of the Victorians.*

This closing is not introducing new evidence: it merely sums up your overall points and should leave the examiner feeling that you have had enough time in the exam to say all that you wanted to say.

For an open book exam, you need to be selective in your preparation and disciplined in the exam. You will be told which books you can take in with you, and it is unlikely that you will be able to make notes in them, although you might be allowed to place markers in the books and/or underline key passages. Be sparing: only mark up those sections that you have identified during your revision as important. Be careful before you mark up anything: make absolutely sure that you are allowed to do this.

In the exam, spending a long time looking for the perfect quote might take too much time away from actually writing your exam answer. When you write essay plans as part of your revision, practise looking up the odd fact or quote, and get into the habit of using the book as sparingly as possible: it is only there for the odd reference or to guide you if you really get stuck.

⏩ Smarter learning

The quotations you choose to memorise will say more than you might expect about how well your revision is deepening your learning. Short quotes that can be used for multiple situations are usually the most useful to you in an exam, but choosing those quotes relies on your expert knowledge of a field and your ability to judge a topic, and potential exam questions, wisely. Once the exams are over, keep these quotes in a safe place so that you can use them again, but also as quick reminders of what you have covered in an area.

Reducing anxiety

Being nervous about an exam is always a good thing: it means that you are ready to go, are keen to succeed and have enough adrenaline in your system to keep your mind sharp. Being *too* nervous, however, can hinder your performance. Your aim is to be nervous but prepared. Your revision tasks will prepare you; the event will make you nervous; the tips below will help to control your nerves.

1 Always know all the practical details of the exam before the day, so that you do not waste your nerves on panicking about where you are going, when and what will happen to you when you get there.

2 Have one or two 'last minute' revision cards with you as you wait to go into the exam. These are the cards that contain information that you simply cannot seem to remember, and will be left outside the room as you go in.

3 Nerves make your mouth dry and uncomfortable: take a water bottle with you into each exam.

4 If your blood sugar is likely to dip too low, have something easy to eat (a banana, raisins, a snack bar), ready for the minutes before the exam.

5 If you are not sleeping well, try a nap after each exam: much better than endless discussions with friends about how well you did.

Relaxation techniques

As you wait to go into an exam, there are some techniques you can use to keep your nerves under control:

1 Sit down with your back straight and your feet slightly apart.
2 Spread your fingers wide and rest them lightly on your thighs.
3 Wiggle your toes: they will probably be bunched up with nerves.
4 Relax your tongue: it is probably sticking to the roof of your mouth.
5 Using your right-hand fingers to press firmly, move from the left-hand side of your neck and then along the top of the left-hand side of your back, just above your shoulder blade.
6 Keep this kneading motion going across your shoulder and down the back of your left arm, right down to your wrist.
7 Repeat this process using your left hand on your right side.
8 Breathe out naturally and just close your mouth. Refuse to breathe until you really feel you have to take a breath, then simply open your mouth without any effort to breathe in. Your diaphragm will do all of the work for you, and you will take a naturally calming, deep breath.

diaphragm →

Taking stock

You are about to move into the final phase of your revision, and you can be proud of what you have achieved so far. All of your hard work is now going to pay off, as it all fits into place.

Day 10

Things to do today

☐ Reduce your revision notes for Section Seven of your material to revision cards.

☐ Reduce Section Eight of your material to revision notes.

☐ Keep reducing your pile of revision cards (as many as you have time to do).

☐ Give yourself a mock exam.

A mock exam moves you on to the next stage of your revision. Planning essays is useful for remembering; a mock exam will:

▶ prepare you for how you might feel in the exam

▶ help you to see how well you remember under pressure

▶ give you a sense of how much you can produce against the clock

▶ help to familiarise you with the process of the exam.

How to give yourself a mock essay exam

1 Allow yourself the correct amount of time to do the mock exam, with no interruptions.

2 Put away every scrap of revision material you have.

3 Answer the exam question to time. It does not matter if you have tackled the question before in your revision: this will feel different because it is timed.

4 Use the time to plan, write and check the answer, just as you would in an exam. So, for an hour's essay exam, you would aim to plan for the first 10 minutes, write for 45 minutes and check for the last 5 minutes.

5 If you get stuck, resolutely push yourself to keep going, just as if you were in an exam.

6 When you have finished, take a break and then go back and check:

   ▸ Did you produce a strong opening and ending?
   ▸ Did your plan work? Did you miss out anything vital?
   ▸ Did you have enough time to finish and check the answer?

Beyond these three points, there is no need to worry too much: even if the answer is not as perfect as you would like, you have mastered the basics of the exam, and the rest will come as you continue to revise.

How to give yourself a mock multiple-choice exam

1 As with the essay exam, put away all of your revision material and just face the question.

2 Some of the questions will be fairly easy for you, and answering these first will give you confidence. Do not be tempted to rush too fast, though: it is easy to lose points by making careless mistakes.

3 For the more challenging questions, you will usually be offered one answer option that is obviously wrong, one that is wrong as soon as you study it in more detail, one that is very nearly right and one that is the correct answer. Focus on these last two.

4 If you are struggling, writing the options out on your scrap paper in the exam can help to clarify things for you.

5 Once you think you have completed the paper, go back and check that you have answered every single question and clearly marked the right box.

6 Finally, check each answer, for both the easier and harder questions, just to make sure that you have not missed anything.

7 Once you have done this: stop. The most dangerous time in a multiple-choice exam is the last minute, when you decide to change several of your answers, and find that you alter your choice to the wrong answer, because you have had time to doubt yourself.

What mock exams do for you

Sometimes you can complete a mock exam and feel elated: it has all gone perfectly and you are delighted with your answer. Sometimes it can leave you despairing. Neither of these is a true response, as both are created from the pressure you have just put on yourself. That is what mock exams are designed to do: get you used to the pressure so that you are less likely to panic when you are in the exam room.

When you come to look back at your mock exam answers, you will find that they are never absolutely right or absolutely wrong; just as in an exam, your performance will differ each time. That is why it is essential to check your mock exam answers as you move forward: to guide you in your revision, but also to remind you how far you have come. Again, keep your know-it gremlin beside you, so that you can be confident about what most of your mock exams will show you: that you have mastered a good part of the material you need.

From now on, you will aim to do mock exams alongside your other revision tasks, so that you keep focused on the ultimate goal: the exam itself.

Things to do today

☐ Reduce your revision notes for Section Eight of your material to revision cards.

☐ Tidy up your work space.

☐ STOP for the day.

This is, deliberately, an easier day than most. You have been working hard, with an increasing number of tasks each day, and you need to take stock. Tidying away your discarded revision cards, filing all of the revision notes you no longer need and throwing away all the rubbish that has accumulated will keep things in control and also clear your head ready for the final push before the exams.

Knowing when and why to stop

Today has been an easier day, giving your brain the chance to relax a little. Like the rest day on Day Seven, your mind will have been assimilating material and sorting it even without you realising it. Going into an exam as a frazzled, exhausted wreck is not going to do you any good: it is better to know a little less and be fresh and ready to use what you do know to maximum effect than to know much more and be too tired to benefit from it.

From now on, you must trust yourself. There will still be revision tasks to do, and you have plenty of time left to master more material, but, if you get tired or find that you are busy getting nowhere, ask yourself these questions:

1 *Is it difficult to focus because, actually, I already know this material?* Be firm with yourself and put it to one side.
2 *Have I just got bored with this task?* Move on to another task and come back to this later.
3 *Have I lost motivation with the whole process?* Take a decent break (several hours, if you need to), and then try again.
4 *Are my nerves stopping me from thinking straight?* This is the perfect time to practise the relaxation techniques from Day Nine.

Things to do today

❑ Make a final check on your revision cards, focusing especially on those you made yesterday.

❑ Keep reducing your pile of revision cards. It will not matter if you cannot do this for all of your revision cards: just review as many as you have time to do.

❑ Make a 'last minute' card (or several) for each section of your material.

❑ Take stock of your position.

How to know how much you know: sorting the cards

In these last couple of days, your key focus is best placed on assessing what you know. There is a system for this:

1 Put the pile of revision cards for each section of material on the table in front of you. Put your 'last minute' cards for each section to one side – you will only need these just before each exam.

2 Some piles will be larger than others, depending on how much you knew already and how much time you have been able to spend reducing each set of cards, but that is no problem.

3 Take the first pile, glance at the title of each card and try reciting what you think is on that card. You are unlikely ever to be perfect at this, and there is no need to be. If you have found another way to test yourself that suits your learning style better, then you will use that method.

4 If you feel you know nearly all of the material on the card, put it on one pile; if you feel much less confident about the contents of the card, put it on another pile.

5 There will probably be a third pile here, too – the cards that you now think are not really essential because they contain material that you do not realistically expect to use in the exam. These are not wasted cards: by making them you have ensured that you know some of the material, enough to refer to it in passing if you need to.

How to know how much you know: mastering the cards

For each section of material, you will now have three piles of cards:

1 The pile of cards with material you have chosen not to use in the exam, except in passing or in an emergency, can be firmly placed to one side.

2 For each section, you can ignore for now the pile of cards where you are confident of the material: you can look at these every now and then tomorrow, and between exams, as a confidence boost and reminder. Keep your know-it gremlin close by you for this: you *do* know this material.

3 With the pile of cards where you are less familiar with the material, check each one and be ruthless: can you realistically expect to remember this card for the exam, and is it essential that you know this material, or should the card be added to your discarded pile?

You are now left with a pile of cards, which you need to tackle head-on …

4 For those cards with material you absolutely have to learn, because you are sure it will come up in the exam or it is part of an area you want to cover, use them as 'flash cards'.

5 For each 'flash card', glance at the title, cover the card, recite the material as best you can, then check how well you have done. There is no easy way to do this and it can be a little tedious, but repeating this process over and over will give you the best chance of remembering the material.

6 Once you feel confident about the material, you can add that card to your pile of cards about which you feel happy.

It is unlikely that you will go into any exam having learnt all of the material on every card, but that will not be a problem: you will have mastered enough material to use it well to produce a good exam answer.

Openings and endings

Beginning an exam answer well and polishing it off with a flourish will always impress examiners. It shows that you have strong ideas, with a clear sense of how to express them, and that you are in control of your subject. They are also a great way to revise in this, the final stage of your revision. To practise, you can use past or sample papers; or, at this stage, you will be able to make up your own questions, similar to those you have worked on before.

1 Give yourself a time limit (probably no more than 15 minutes).
2 There is no need to make a full plan, but brainstorm your answer if you feel it will help.
3 Write out just the opening paragraph – use bullet points to make your ideas clearer if this makes it easier.
4 Write out your ending to the answer – this might be no more than a sentence or two, summing up what you would have covered.

In those 15 minutes or so, you have reminded yourself of the area, decided how to tackle it and effectively revised it, all in one swift exercise.

Some people find strong openings and endings easy, whilst others struggle a bit. By writing out a few of these in the day before each exam you will feel far more confident as you face each question.

Taking stock

You have done nearly all you can now to ensure your success. Although you will keep working your material to boost your confidence, from now on it is much more about achieving focus, being firm in your aims and clear about what you are doing. So it is important to take a moment to acknowledge what you have achieved so far:

Things to do today

☐ Make a final check on the exam arrangements: the time, the place and how you will get there. This sounds so simple, but it is far too easy to get something wrong.

☐ Keep on looking at your revision cards, to brush up on some final material.

☐ Practise openings and endings for exam answers.

☐ Buy some high-energy snacks for tomorrow.

☐ Plan to take a night off, if you can.

And the first thing to do in the exam is …

On the day before the exam it is a good idea to make clear in your mind now exactly how you will face the beginning of an exam:

▶ Remember how you aimed to divide your time between planning, writing and checking – if you have an hour for each essay, ideally 10 minutes planning, 45 minutes writing, and 5 minutes checking. Remember that other types of exams might require significant alterations in this timing.

▶ Read ALL the questions twice, putting a star beside the ones you think you want to answer. Do not be afraid to ask the invigilators if you think there is something wrong with the paper.

▶ If the paper is multiple-choice, use the strategy outlined on Day Ten.

▶ Unburden your mind of all the 'rubbish' that will get in the way – do this by jotting down the material from your 'last minute' card.

▶ Read the questions again, confirming your choice.

▶ Remember how any mock exams you gave yourself felt at this point: this will help to calm your nerves and focus your mind.

▶ Decide, in advance of the exam if you can, whether you will plan each answer at the beginning or plan each essay as you work through the paper.

- Decide, in advance of the exam, whether it will be better for you to answer your 'strongest' question first or last.
- For each question:
    - Make a six-point plan straight away of your key points: this might be a brainstorm or just a list (3 minutes).
    - Read the question again.
    - 'Flesh out' your six-point plan using your preferred planning method (7 minutes). Does it still make sense? At this stage, include a note of some details that you plan to include, such as quotes, dates, references, chemical symbols or formulae, and so forth.
    - Go back to your 'rubbish dump' and see if anything from there needs to be included.
- Only now do you begin to write, or perhaps to plan your other answers. This takes courage. Many of the people around you will already be scribbling away madly; hold your nerve and write only when you are sure you are ready to go … your answers will be better for it.

The night before the exam

What to do ... .

It is easy to *say* 'Plan to take the night off' – it is far harder to do this in reality. Remember that by now you will have all the material you are likely to be able to retain already in your head: endlessly going over and over it will make little difference.

If you know you might work yourself into a frenzy of nerves to no good purpose the night before an exam, it might be a good idea to plan a relaxed evening out with friends, perhaps with an activity that will distract you nicely.

If you know that being completely away from your work will be more stressful than not, then give yourself the easiest possible revision time by just having some of your most important revision cards beside you as you try to relax. That way, you can always reassure yourself of how far you have come, and this will help to keep you calm.

What not to do …

Try not to leave your evening entirely unplanned. If you have no idea how you are going to occupy your time, you are more likely to drift about in a state of anxiety.

Look after yourself physically. An excess of food or alcohol or a late night is likely to impair your performance.

Avoid any discussion at all about the exam with anyone else who is taking it. If you realise you need to know a specific detail about the practicalities, do check it, but talking at length about the exam is more likely to scare than to comfort you. At this stage, rumours about the exam and what is required of you will be flying about, and will only unnerve you.

Go offline if you can – scare stories will lurk there and can be hugely distracting and often distressing at this stage. If you know that you will not rest until you have made one final check of the practical arrangements for tomorrow, you could ask a friend to do it for you to remove the temptation of browsing into disaster.

Day 14: exam day!

Things to do today

❑ Eat something – anything – to prepare you for the day ahead. If you cannot manage a full meal, snack on foods that will keep your energy levels high.

❑ Aim to get to the exam room no more than thirty minutes before the exam. This will give you time to check that it is the right place, so that you can wander off for a while, but much longer than this waiting around will just increase your nerves.

❑ If you need reassurance, check over your 'last minute' card for the exam, and remind yourself of the plan of attack outlined below.

In the exam …

Before you start to write

Think back to the exam strategies outlined in Day One, so that you feel confident about the order in which you will answer the questions, the way you can best answer them and the planning approach that suits you for this type of exam.

When you are writing

▶ Work from your detailed plan, but keep an eye on the time. Be prepared to abandon a point in the best way you can if you are running too far over on time, but allow it to flow naturally for as long as you can.

▶ If you have to leave a point, leave enough space so that you can direct the marker to work that you add later on.

▶ If you get desperate on time, you might need to direct the marker back to your plan so that it is clear where you would have gone had you been given more time.

If you wobble

▶ Several peculiar things can happen to your brain in an exam:
  ▶ You seem to be writing complete rubbish.
  ▶ You lose the point of what you wanted to say.
  ▶ You start to doubt that you have answered the right question.

In fact, these are unlikely to be real problems, in that none of them will be a true reflection of the situation. What is really happening is that you are getting tired, or nerves are getting the better of you, or you have just had to go through too many exams in a short space of time. If this happens to you, STOP WRITING for a few seconds, take a breath and check your plan. This will ground you back in your main six points, and the whole process will become easier again.

 14 DAYS TO EXAM SUCCESS

- If, in the few seconds that you have taken a break, you decide that you really *have* gone off course, close the point you are making as soon as you can and move firmly on to your next point. This will ensure that you keep on track.

And towards the end …

- Checking is always going to be important, but you have relatively little time to do this in an exam. If you have five minutes, you will have time to read your whole script through for errors and inconsistency. This would be a better choice than simply continuing to write until the very end of the exam.
- If you are running out of time, and have only a few minutes to do some final checking, abandon the idea of reading through the entire script and instead look for typical weak points in each answer:
  - *The opening:* does it say what you mean?
  - *The conclusion:* is it strong enough?
  - *Titles and dates:* are they accurate?
  - *Names, figures, formulae and topic-specific terms:* are they right?
  - *Blanks and spaces:* can you fill them in now?
  - *Gaps left for more writing:* do you have time now?
  - *Between two-thirds and three-quarters of the way through:* did you have a moment of madness, where you made an odd mistake that you can now correct?

And when it is over …

Forget it! You know that you have worked hard for this exam. If you have a specific concern (did I get a particular fact right?) then you might check it with a couple of friends, but, beyond that, post mortems are rarely a good idea.

The following day, however, you might like to reflect upon your strengths and weaknesses whilst they are fresh in your mind. Make a note of what you intend to do differently in future exams. It is surprising how quickly the details of the experience fade from your mind, but notes made now will help you to focus your energy in future exams.

If you have several days between exams, follow the steps on Days Twelve and Thirteen to keep your mind ticking over, but make sure you build some decent rest breaks into your schedule.

You are here because you deserve to be. Contrary to popular belief, exams are an exciting time – you are finally getting the chance to show how well you have grasped your subject. You will do your best and produce the results that you need …

Good Luck!

Index